loretta's song

a collection of poetry by

t. kilgore splake

p.o. box 508
calumet, michigan 49913

© t.k. splake 2010. All rights reserved and nothing may be copied, electronically transmitted or used in any way without author's written consent, with the exception of brief passages quoted in reviews.

ISBN 978-1-4507-3295-6

Printed in the United States of America by Gage Printing Company
220 Buckner Drive, Battle Creek, Michigan 49037
First Edition, First Printing, August 2010

dedicated to
loretta magner

LORETTA A. MAGNER   2/26/01

Loretta A. Magner, 88 of Three Rivers, died Friday, February 23, 2001 at Bowman House, in Three Rivers. Born April 13, 1912 in St. Johns, Michigan to Edward J. and Susie (Cramer) Magner. Miss Magner graduated and received degrees from both Eastern Michigan University (B.A.) as well as the University of Michigan (M.A.). She taught school in Shiawassee County for two years, Palo for one year, Delton Kellogg for eight years and at Three Rivers High School for 30 years. After her retirement in 1974 she substituted in Three Rivers Schools. Throughout her life she was a member of Delta Kappa Gamma, American Association of University Women, honorary member of the Three Rivers Womens Club, Three Rivers Hospital Auxiliary, M.E.A., N.E.A., N.R.T.A. and Immaculate Conception Church.

Surviving is a sister Velma Jarrad of Lansing, Michigan. Two brothers John (Joyce) Magner of Eaton Rapids, Michigan, James (Norma) Magner of Washington and several nieces and nephews.

A Celebration of Life Mass will be held at 11 a.m. Saturday, March 10, 2001 at Immaculate Conception Church in Three Rivers. Father Matthew Illikattil of Immaculate Conception Church will co-celebrate the Mass with Father Michael Hazard of St. Joseph Church in Kalamazoo. A private burial will take place in Bethany Cemetery, Morrice, Michigan. The family asks those wishing to give memorials please remember Immaculate Conception School or charity of one's choice, envelopes are available at the funeral home. Arrangements by Halverson Chapel.

introduction

late one afternoon after my high school classes, a smith family friend, karl millard, stopped by the house and asked if i wanted to go for a ride. i politely thanked karl and said no, but immediately i knew my father had died. i was a sophomore when emery had his fatal heart attack and it was difficult for me to understand just what i had lost. i remember feeling ashamed for not ever having a dad like the rest of the high school students. i also recall after his death my mother asking my sisters why i didn't cry at the funeral. margaret was frequently telling me "emery isn't around anymore to get you out of trouble."

for the next two years i sleep-walked through my classes with average grades. in my free time, i watched television, played swamp hockey with the guys from constantine, and fished the three rivers. when i became a high school senior, i didn't have any serious idea about what i wanted to do after graduation. i knew i didn't want to become a paper mill lifer, putting in forty-hour weeks and drinking the weekends away. also, when i was seventeen, going to college did not seem like an attractive idea.

following a bitter weekend of arguments with my mother, i cut my monday classes and hitch-hiked to kalamazoo to talk with the navy recruiter. after passing the navy entrance exam without missing a question, i decided to quit three rivers, abandon the "class of 1955," study photography in the navy, and get my high school diploma after boot camp. this decision also would leave my disagreements with margaret far behind me.

after my perfect test score, the kalamazoo navy recruiter strongly urged me to finish school and get a diploma before joining the navy. having burned my bridges in three rivers, i stayed with my oldest sister, catherine, to finish high school at kalamazoo central.

the difference between three rivers high school and kalamazoo central was startling. the upjohn and gilmore community influences wanted the best for the city of kalamazoo. so central high school was probably the best school system in the state of michigan in the 1950's.

the senior boys had college applications for yale, harvard, and princeton, while the senior girls were anxious to get accepted at vassar, wellesley, barnard, or another ivy league college.

i still remember the late nights spent memorizing spanish stories for helen grable's class. in physics class i built a radio for teacher roy mesick and wrote a research paper explaining radio technology. my radio construction was done in the earlier period of aluminum chassis, glass radio tubes, and super-heterodyne electronics. in elf pedler's senior studies class i gave a speech explaining how i hoped to become a photographer after joining the navy. finally, in mary william's english class, she would tease john chumus and myself about not being able to "guess" the right answers on the grammar exams.

after passing my college preparatory classes at kalamazoo central, i chose not to attend the three rivers high school baccalaureate service or the cap-and-gown graduation ceremony. to teach tommy a lesson in middle-class morals and manners, superintendent oscar horst and principal edmund blank refused to give me my high school diploma. this was the anal retentive rigidity of the 50's "father knows best" mentality.

the kalamazoo navy recruiter talked the superintendent and principal into finally giving me my high school diploma from the three rivers school system.

looking back today, it doesn't seem strange that i feel i am really a graduate of kalamazoo central, where i worked so hard to pass my classes and learn, rather than the three-plus years i merely existed in the three rivers schools.

as a young teenager, i quickly discovered the power of walking the walk as well as talking the talk. i learned well the role and voice of the outsider, watching marlon brando in "the wild one," and james dean in "rebel without a cause." i found satisfaction in questioning my life's situations and the strength gained in arriving at my own answers.

the single warm memory i have of my three rivers school years was loretta magner, my english and latin teacher. in her *three rivers commercial* obituary it said that loretta "was very respected by students and faculty,...and she was always friendly."

during my school years i bought senior scholastic paperback books from miss magner, including one of my still favorite titles, *starbuck valley winter*. in eleventh grade english class she would frequently praise my short stories and read them to the rest of the students. loretta also managed to pass me for two years in latin, which was a most kind gesture. she also had a plaque and in my front row seat, every day i read:

>today is the tomorrow
>you're worried about yesterday
>all is well
>smile
>
>(anonymous author)

finally, when emery died, and i was wondering about my life and what to do with it, loretta was the only person in three rivers to send me a sympathy card. many years later i escaped battle creek, michigan, and my position as a college professor at kellogg community college. i retired to munising, in michigan's upper peninsula to write poetry for the rest of my life.

on one beer-laced evening, i remembered the kindness of loretta and checked the three rivers phone directory and found her telephone number. loretta and i had a long and fine conversation, filling in the tom smith gaps since i had left three rivers high school.

following our phone chatting, the rat bastard time of passing years vanished quickly. as i became a gray beard poet, loretta passed away in february 2001, at the age of 88 in three rivers.

russian writer and film director andrei tarkovsky in his movie "stalker" said "when man thinks of his past he becomes kinder." "loretta's song" is a collection of my poetry dedicated to my increasingly warm memories of miss magner. if she is indeed a spirit somewhere in our cosmos, i hope that she finds a verse or three here to enjoy.

margaret

like all mothers
always knowing everything
one evening asking
"what's wrong
with being tom smith"

ghost bard

homemade book of poems
dusty "used store" shelf
forgotten love dreams
someone's soul
waiting

new life

quitting slavery
missing freedom
name on shirt
times doing nothing
when things simpler

fellini's roma

ancient roman frescoes
exposed to light
slowly fading
other people's lives
history disappearing

life

job preference test
personality choice
select one of the following
actor
artist
hero
outlaw

chairman

all but dissertation
npr and *new yorker* cartoons
pbs special features
unable to understand
brautigan stories and poems
"cleveland wrecking yard"
selling trout streams
five dollars a foot
while i laugh
wet happy tears

brain-skull blindness

safe sad ignorance
forgotten prisoner
cold black hole
endless nada mas
dry leaves whisper
scrapping tree bark
sudden reminder
energy flowing
through living things
beauty love
found inside

another night passing

weather channel news
good people
fighting killer storms
endless hours
watching b+w movies
old fred astaire films
afterwards
ashes and bones
undertaker's urn
talking to mother again
until first dawn

spring

old t.s. was wrong
eliot's *the waste land*
april is not the cruelest month
breeding lilacs memory desire
graybeard poet
"long white" survivor
alive to witness
bask in another
ice out
blood bath
sense of beginning

the stranger

pudeur
espresso
café flore vino
gauloises
fresh croissants
le panelier study
solidaire
solitaire
final
peaceful
innocence

memories

young boy
fat tire bike
baseball card collection
marsh wheeling box
rare clyde klutz prize
st lou brownie uniform
remembering bb-gun kill
dead robin feathers
later finding
smooth bony skull
now graying man
like dead tree
awaiting next storm

mother

still saving margaret's
wooden potato masher
baking rolling pin
huge yellow ceramic bowl
mixing dish
for holiday recipes
cookies cakes pies
mom's turquoise china lamp
torn and battered shade
lighting my bardic corner
early mornings
when i chase
my always elusive
dame lady muse

epiphany

warming campfire coals
growing first light shadows
black coffee cooling
early morning chill
burned-out professor
nursing modest hangover
remembering past day or three
catching brook trout limit
black bear in camp
fantastic lightning thunder storm
hooting at owls
coaxing one to visit
writing things down
memo-book pages
my first poems

growing up

mother reading me
little red riding hood
peter rabbit tales
first grade primer
dick jane spot
look look
see the funny animal
ted mike casey
kids finding sesame street
bert ernie bigbird
abcs counting to ten
now graybeard climbing **cliffs**
seeking rogue coyote
seeking wisdom
in deep yellow eyes

untitled brautigan

sleeping late
with van girl susie
smoking breakfast dope
making love
drinking bottle or two of champagne
making love again
somehow baking "weed brownies"
in tin foil
on coleman camp stove
thinking while wrestling naked
we were like alonzo hagen's
"trout fishing in america diary"
each toke
slug of icy brut
trippy chocolate square
was another fishing trip
more trout lost

late autumn psychosis

sad forever boy
like holden caulfield
lost in others' imagination
wanting safe childhood life
lacking real world persona
high school nobody
majoring in band
last chair clarinet spaz
never hearing woman say
"love you need you"
marriage kids steady job
health insurance pension
impossible mad dreams
dad says he loves him
doesn't need any help
brings new comic books home
basement home retreat
gray november morning
huge snowflakes
falling fast and staying

ghost

nightly riding "the dog"
md 20-20 buzzz
eagles ballads on stereo
low volume sound
distant soothing hummm
"take it to the limit"
remembering john fante
once passionate artist
now forgotten ashes
yet still we ask
does life have meaning
waiting early morning
fewer competing distractions
hot plate coffee
hammering new courier
twelve-point font
peaceful writing escape
hoping epiphanic moment
ohhhhhhhh please
"one more time"

after birth

last night's
warm pbr breakfast
like consul finney
under the volcano hangover
brain blowtorch meltdown
distant shimmering vision
wild unshaven beard
burnt black acres
forest fire debris
nobody loves you
hurt angry loss
empty solitude
certain
there is no god
afterlife salvation
time to become
mysterious bo ho beatster
waiting hoping
one good day
writing new poem
everyone will remember

it's time

sunday afternoon chest pain
nerves or indigestion
or cardiac attack symptoms
living alone
urgent fears growing
panic rush
go to hospital emergency
instead sit and die
or have serious stroke
brain-dead nobody
talking with other vegetables
remembering dad's fatal coronary
big muscle blow
scared resigned angry
sound and light fading
falling into darkness
face in carpet shag
waiting voice of god
visions of heaven
peaceful afterlife
wife and tommy
mourning his passing
choosing eulogy words

valentine's day

two morning hsitzz's
married with mouths
conglomerate café ethiopian
hot ceramic cups
kids long gone
husbands distant memory
alone nights
cold empty beds
middle-aged double chins
messy graying hair
thanksgiving christmas
extra holiday pounds
bullet-proofed hearts
denying love
man's hungry bones
mysterious sweet fucking
ecstatic loss of being
low calorie yogurts
babette's blueberry muffins
home to watch
weather channel hours
today's special
"tornado fascination"

graybeard essence

aging college professor
slow death retreat
sick of crazy world
mad people
chasing dollars
loveless sexual disappointments
becoming a poet
sleeping on gym mat
hot plate stove
metal sink enamel rusted
share bath and toilet
down the hall
bardic musings at
abandoned freda smelter ruins
wind scarred superior shore
acting as sisyphus
climbing ancient **cliffs**
chasing truth
finding inner quiet
living in spiritual light
keweenaw peninsula
warm lightness like
rome and florence sun
final days recalling
dying and rebirth

no one caring

heavy powder dusting
morning white ghost
fresh hairdo
fancy sunday clothes
tv weather channel news
home alone pause
conglomerate café coffee
looking for a friend
older children grown
living in distant parts
loose wedding ring
tiny bony finger
bird feeder filled
cat fed
no mail today
nothing to do
lacking new ideas
exciting fresh words
blank page always empty
without librium
lithium or alcohol relief
whispers growing louder
"you should go"
back to vacant house
awaiting quiet death

panic attacks

aging professional student
latest sad excuse
failing quizzes and exams
unfinished research papers
still living
outside 'real world' demands
older past friends
already moving on
jobs marriages families
raising young kids
living with his parents
hovering helicopter
controlling mother and father
late nights
watching "wheel of fortune" reruns
television sound off
greedy fat lady
screaming over dollars won
wrinkled newspaper horoscopes
on the floor
full of tomorrow's
successes and good fortunes
taking a piss
checking bathroom mirror
looking for bald spot
just like dad

beyond the waterfall

cheap old milwaukee suds
bushmills shots
angels softly singing
mad rush in
brain-skull cavity
sweet delicious sin
waking after surgery
heart rhythm fix
cold turkey rehab
never serious question
quiet new existence
unlike papa hem
failing sawtooth ghosts
brautigan going belly up
dead like sixties dream
hunter thompson
declaring nada mas
good stuff and booze
now seeking
mountain lion shadow
cool early morning mists
following dusty prints
path to granite summit
learning secrets
gaining wisdom
life above
beyond passing clouds

quiet desperation

retiring college professor
smaller payday checks
silently leaving
daily classroom lectures
campus celebrity status
indifferent student minds
blackboard erasers
dusty chalk tray remains
no longer true believer
doubting self
precious subject matter
desire to be something
losing to
can't take it anymore
too late for new dreams
solitary loneliness
without another to love
nyquil jack daniel's days
watching t.v. soaps
"young and restless"
"one life to live"
nights with pbr chasers
catching poker players
espn early a.m. returns
others taking chances
walking the walk
talking the talk
retired poet
creative canvas blank
notebook pages empty
nada mas nada mas

seconds hours days
waiting on some stranger
covering him with earth

springtime memories

early morning dawn
staining eastern horizon
luminescent shimmer
lac la belle tides
solitary angler
working weedy shallows
quietly stalking
trophy tiger trout
distant sandhill cranes
squawking misty shadows
guarding nests
spring baby birds
sunday a.m. predator
seeking easy breakfast
awkward "v" formations
returning keweenaw geese
louisiana wintering
early mia spaces
gaggle members lost
fisherman staring skyward
like general savage
b-17's returning
framlington airfield
"12 o'clock high"
wounded planes and flyers
"bloody 100th wing"
gregory peck
remembering squadron ghosts
bishop cobb wilson zimmy
exploding flak
fw-109 nightmare casualties

toby mug
evening bar hours
wanting and waiting
time to go home

ghost road

mother and father
fleeing poor michigan farms
acres bankers owned
like midwestern orphan train
"placed out" kids
escaping starving slavery
raised in methodist "goodness"
white bread americana
taught sex not delightful
sunday visits to cemetery
visiting relatives graves
dad always working
money buying class
mom pushing culture
piano lessons high school band
rare summer family picnics
sandwiches and lemonade
pressed to get a job
move ahead
reading books
watching movies
finding my real self
writing poems
what i was born for
young boy
suddenly old man
not believing in heaven
empty eulogy words
waiting morphine narrative
or .357 wisdom
wondering what happened

to ancient family album
faded sepia photos
smith and anderson past ancestry
garage sale bargain
vanished in dumpster
some dusty archive shelf

camus

facel vega crash
outside petit villeblevin
silencing *combat's* voice
his innocent french *pudeur*
no more
café flore breakfasts
espresso and fresh croissants
later deux magots
smoky gauloise discussions
pursuing artistic truth
graying sisyphus
climbing mountain paths
above le panelier studio
collecting paniers of wild mushrooms
visiting almond orchards
walking in olive groves
sipping tart thimbleberry wine
once algerian poet
finding inner peace
in ancient mediterranean ruins
windswept coast vegetation
leaving other writers
painful creative blocks
new poem story book worries
loving twins
daughter catherine son jean
maria casares
les enfants du paradis mistress
mysterious mi
girl wearing black pajamas
bright orange slippers

their spiritual innocence
lightness of being
with invisible summer sun
warming winter depths
forever two
young souls

paris memories

hemingway's
saw mill apartment
notre-dames-des-champs
one decent suit
respectable pair of shoes
generation perdue
lost generation poet
not trusting non-veterans
deux magots *café au lait*
zinc bar cheap vino
seeking one true sentence
another and another
talking with seine fishermen
angling *goujon* dinner
horse chestnut rabbit's foot
good luck charms
disciplined schedule
born to create books
hating wasted days
empty notebook pages
"pilot fish and rich"
ruining *a moveable feast*
best place to work
their every day fiestas
collecting lazy friends
while searching for new place
schruns mountain lodge
winter skiing vacation
hadley's stolen suitcase
gare de lyon station
short stories gone

life moving on
loving marrying
pauline martha mary
spanish civil war
battle of hurtgen forest
african safaris
hunting wild animals
open veldt expanse
fishing gulf stream currents
pilar sailfish days
old man and the sea
floridita "papa doubles"
finca working retreat
"city of lights"
final chapter
sawtooth mountain shadows

point betsy

early morning **cliffs** climb
drizzle changing to snow
winter weather storm warning
tonight into tomorrow
sliding down escarpment ledge
with red tibetan prayer flag
fastened to pine tree bough
long winter reminder
for sister mary
remembering christmas morning
smith family home
lifetime or three ago
mary taking me downstairs
tree lights shining
warm kubrick glow
presents wrapped and waiting
"thank you" note from santa
for cookies and coke
nighttime holiday treat
growing up in
lively competitive household
mary setting impossible challenges
college degrees
michigan columbia yale
ph-d dissertation
becoming published book
giving fine arts lectures
to argentine and german scholars
finally failing
fleeing rat bastard time
mary suddenly gone

red flag still flying
atop **cliffs** granite summit
providing brother tommy
season of "long white" respect
while writing
new poems
short story collections
another book manuscript
credit silently passing
sister mary's
long gray shadow

snow fevers

saturday overnight
long white accumulation
softening metrops
later sunday morning
weightless snow flurries
blurring past memories
occasional bard 'res' creaking
ancient timbers settling
graybeard poet
consciousness rising
waking from deep slumber
like swimming
under water
moving up
toward the surface
silent dreamy flashbacks
9/11 falling man
big apple smoking towers
going to hell statement
auschwitz jewish prisoner
dancing on electric wire
concentration camp perimeter
waldheim and glass
waffen "ss" guards
stiff gray uniforms
double rune ornaments
homeless small children
searching lost parents
nagasaki hiroshima rubble
black rain falling
swiss ex-pat wife

empty valium bottle bedside
padlocked hospital room
hearing olga say
"you son-of-a-bitch"
leaving no doubt
love dead
marriage over
life never getting better

poet

early morning
shaking of zzzz's
tossing couchin' it blankets
toes sticking out of
holes in red socks
graybeard artist
bard 'res' sanctuary
superman's
fortress of solitude
batcave and blackhawk island
escapist's "key hole"
under empire state building
rice madness stew
cooling in crockpot
hot plate turkey legs warming
shredded bran-wheat squares
spoon-sized snacks
basic bardic diet
without salt sugar fat
solitary scribe
beyond true romance
leaving love to movies
poontang desires
left to past lifetimes
viagra "blue bomber"
waiting for smart
mature knowing woman
twenty-one year old tranny
ancient dodge la strata
steady dependable wheels
no wild dreams

classy lamborghini
small mind plaything
reclusive rogue
not giving a damn
never traveling
seeing different places
meeting other people
instead leaving society
to know-nothing pretenders
those watching tv soap operas
sit-com reruns
late nights
trickster coyote hunter
chasing dangerous prey
brain-skull cavity imaginations
measuring existential conflicts
lightness darkness
in real world contests
no more alcoholic courage
xanax lexapro valium help
writer's block excuses
regardless of serotonin levels
testosterone and dark rainy
far north dreariness
daily wrestling elusive
damn dame lady muse
writing new
poems and stories
tommy splake smith
dream book manuscript
early winter mornings
climbing **cliffs**
warm wool watch cap

snug against ears
welcome witness to cool
salmon-violet sunrise
now and then
leaning into clippers
fresh buzzzzz-job
pushing back pale beard
yearly near-terminal
spring motorcycle fevers
always surviving
daily metrops post grabbery
mailbox incoming
waiting new netflix film
next ammo-zon
single-click book order
always knowing if cubs won
how celts did
new york giants michigan wolverines
game time scores
once laughing at hem
now thinking papa was right
life and poetry
should be damn straight

come in rangoon

holter monitor lines
revealing dangerous arrhythmia
serious problem
with big heart muscle
graybeard poet telling
local doctor
"i will not"
take ambulance trip
riding to marquette hospital
cardiovascular specialists
young tommy
growing up with
generation of "flying tigers"
not afraid of dying
like "pappy" boyington
"blacksheep" mac mcgarry
aces chasing jap zeroes
protecting burma road
wearing leather jackets
chinese flag
with "blood chit"
message for help
if shot down
flying claire chennault's
p-40's with tiger teeth
kumming yunfu luichow
my artful dodger
turning steady miles
engine smooth hummm
like warm cockpit
relaxed hand on throttle

earplugs goggles oxygen mask
wondering about god
survival of one's soul
thinking of love
young girls lost
married women divorced
sons and daughter
mother and father memories
determined survivor
toughing out whatever
getting surgery
returning to
god's country home
rehabbing quickly
still time to write
new novel manuscript
quiet season of "long white"
early winter mornings
contesting ever elusive
damn dame lady muse
one more time

magnum

city limits fading
rearview mirror shadows
easy quiet miles
early morning darkness
memory drifting back
late night years ago
brain-skull cavity numb
cheap old milwaukee suds
holding .357
remembering scary stories
others saying
"violent recoil
smashed the gun in his face"
carefully squeezing trigger
fiery barrel explosion
red line of poetry
aimed toward heaven
maybe
killing god
wounding angel or two
scattering milky way
this morning
testing ancient gun
insuring no malfunction
like empty hammer click
moment of truth
when seriously needing
holy ticket to ride
trip to new reality
standing besides brautigan creek
trailhead start to **cliffs**

aiming at distant trees
avoiding
"no not now"
fatal ricochet mistake
smith-wesson exploding
earth shaking tremor
poor rock gravel
moving beneath my feet
suddenly head
feeling full of cotton
silently thinking
"eh eh eh
can't hear anything"
in blurry first dawn
thinking
of other writers
alone and unloved
lost in mind-fuck depression
also knowing
when words vanish
nothing else remains
except final goodbye
existential poetic adieu
randall jarrell
walking into car
north carolina highway
weldon kees
leaping off
san francisco
golden gate bridge
lew welch
leaving gary snyder's cabin
california mountains

with 30-30 rifle
body never found
brother brautigan rotting
bolinas west coast apartment
now trout fishing
absaroka mists
dreaming of ianthe
watermelon sugars
old papa hem
dazed vacant stare
sawtooth mountains too close
toes in shotgun triggers
young beloved adriana
patiently waiting
somewhere across the river
david foster wallace
putting rope around his neck
hanging himself
while faithful canine companions
"bella" and "warner"
watching
not understanding
truth finally setting him free
my .357 magic
warm and smoky
field tested
ready to go
passing single bullet agony
hot violent end
some time
not far away
when failure and decay
reach beyond my life
erasing new poem

special place

young henry darger
mother father dead
brothers sisters adopted
placed in catholic boy's home
saint augustine church mission
lincoln illinois
doctor's diagnosis
"little henry's heart
not in the right place"
escaping lincoln asylum
walking to chicago
witnessing huge tornado
tremendous winds destroying
barns windmills farm buildings
one-room second floor apartment
west webster avenue
chicago's north side
shabby dressed recluse
hospital janitor job
washing floors and windows
working year upon year
before retirement
collecting old newspapers and magazines
discarded comic books
pepto-bismol bottles
making balls of string
accumulating other's garbage
henry's precious belongings
five-year old elsie paroubek
kidnapped and murdered
becoming his *magnum opus*

dedicating his lifetime
to saving unprotected children
imaginary robert vivian
seven young daughters
rebelling against john manley
glandelinian regime's
horrible child slavery
vivian's war
writings and drawings
in twelve massive volumes
in the realm of the unreal
hero-leader darger
with seven vivian sisters
fighting to defeat glandelinians
bringing victory to christianity
freeing all children
to be happy
safe from abuse
able to dream
go to school
darger's death in 1973
ended the glandelinian conflicts
vivan girl's determined crusade
henry's books
remarkable watercolor paintings
small room cramped artistry
suddenly silent
modest cemetery headstone epitaph
"artist"
"protector of children"
janet new zealand daughter
impoverished railroad engineer
brother with epilepsy

two younger sisters drowning
"seacliff lunatic asylum" patient
other psychiatric hospital stays
over 200 electro-therapy shocks
the lagoon and other stories
"hubert church memorial award"
canceling lobotomy surgery
later book
owls do cry
frame called local dump
"a treasure"
afraid of hospitals and doctors
janet immigrated to
iziza andorra english homes
to prevent another forced asylum stay
new writings explaining schizophrenia
"fear sane have of the mad"
to the is-land
describing london flat
weather reports books new manuscripts
way for entering
her "special view"
place beyond herself
moving back in history
passing previous rhythms
reaching the beginning
lightness of birth
death's darkness
asked about bach classics
she replied "i can see it"
their creative location
quiet and alone
feeling more alive

realizing exciting energies
other voices had forgotten
henry free
to wage magnificent war
fight bitter battles
with seven vivian daughters
resisting glandelinian power
enslavement and torture of children
reclusive janet
living as mysterious migratory bird
measuring sun's auras
black cloudy shadows
seeking place without borders
poet's safe home

my escape

nightmare years ago
laying .357 down
deciding not to stop time
finally giving last lecture
forgetting government and politics
right left liberal conservative
bardic pilgrim moving north
jeans beard leather vest
writing new poetry
often remembering boyhood world
yellow spring daffodils
farming cornfields
swimming naked huffman dam
white apple blossoms
colorful autumn leaves
smoky evening bonfires
first light snowflakes
starting new season of long white
not like wheelers
april and john's paris dream
choosing not to choose
instead deciding
"we can be happy here"
living in three rivers
small michigan village
downtown commercial center
where people bought
food clothing furniture hardware
theaters beauty parlors barbers
coffee shops and restaurants
meeting halls of

elks kiwanis odd fellows
quiet 1950's without
drugs gangs school shootings
day's classroom beginning
with "lord's prayer" and bible reading
becoming dedicated christians
young life regulated by bells
my generation accepting
marriage sex raising children
neighborhood friendliness
families getting together
celebrating vacations and holidays
trying to be happy as parents
without explaining "facts of life"
instead discussing
same old things
weather sport scores price of food
bills bills bills
white bread america
following love's dull toil
daily up and off to work
names sewed under shirt pocket
worker bees society
minimum wage slavery
ward you lived in
determined social class
important growing up factor
contraband machine cigarettes
tom sneaking a smoke
not inhaling
inviting quiet whispers
"that's emery smith's son"
our little town

small to outside world
everything balanced by business dollar
collecting big little book library
five and dime store allowances
winter coats from j.c. penney's
pneumatic tubes whizzing brass canisters
carrying change and receipt
to hidden store treasury
young teenagers growing up
jones saturday night square dancing
drawn to seductive "doo-wop" sounds
elvis chuck berry "fats" domino
dairy bar hangout
small jukeboxes in each booth
later talking about being a man
young life possibilities
three rivers truck stop tables
over hot black coffee
poorer living in factory wards
paper mill chemical wastes
polluting all three rivers
rich bitch bastards
fancy neighborhood homes
golfing memberships
piano lesson demands
playing etudes and sonatas
sheet music inside the bench
three rivers little affected
by 1930's depression
world war two german japanese battles
millions died elsewhere
bombs never fell on us
tommy playing with toy tanks

pretend guns and ammo
while time has vanished
gone gone gone
now beautiful young girls fat
or white-haired bony crones
not worried about being attractive
school sport stars
suffering coronary fibrillations
wearing hospital bracelets
watching iv dribbles
hopping green monitor lines
our mothers and fathers dead
cemetery headstone dates
kids still saving their belongings
air raid captain's cap
push lawn mower
scissor blades underneath
wood working tools
mason jars with red rubber rings
wooden spoons and heavy mixing bowls
cheap costume jewelry
graduating seniors
believing "tomorrow depends on you"
close to aluminum walker days
yet small town's
"sheltering appeal"
nourishing those needing to belong
valentines and st. patrick clovers
may day front porch baskets
memorial day july 4th parades
thanksgiving feastings
santa's christmas morning surprises
while annoyed class organizers

upset by those
school graduates
not coming home to visit
three rivers reunion
aging graybeard retiree
feeling world taken care of
doesn't need me
i can let it go
using neighbor's computer
world-wide web connections
google answering
travel questions
nagging trivia issues
"stardust" on the stereo
vitalis and vitamins
bathroom cabinet ledge
last week's "people" handy
soft lawn chair
blue viagra pill
waiting

lost whisper

blood son
american patriotic hero
strange gene chromosome mix
mother margaret father emery
egg sperm collision
red, white and blue worship
growing in amniotic sea
lonely brave cowboy
military uniform mindset
socialized by ruth hoppin
classroom teachers
three rivers elementary school
"childe" tommy
deep puritan ethic
attending church
sunday school
summer bible lessons
believing discipline and courage
separated men from boys
freed one from cowardice
young boy
destined to become
soldier sailor flying ace
earning battle ribbons
frontline fighting
likely dying in rocket's red glare
december 8, 1936 birthday
dream fantasies of spanish civil war
lincoln brigade rifleman
fighting franco's nationalist troops
bloody jarama valley campaign

witnessing german luftwaffe
"condor legion" messerschmitts
strafing guernica civilians
meeting gellhorn and hemingway
madrid's florida hotel reporters
visiting george orwell
wounded by fascist sniper
in catalonia hospital
also republican soldier
shot in capa photo
later drinking with
bob and gerda taro
small town boy
reading stories seeing movies
watching bogart
rick's "casablanca" nightclub
describing gestapo cruelty
brave european resistance
setting stage for d-day
"gold" "juno" "sword" "utah" "omaha"
normandy invasion beaches
charles yeager
p-51 mustang ace
destroying fw-109's
general frank savage
sending b-17's
hazardous daylight missions
bombing german factories
american g.i. soldiers
racing over lundendorff bridge
crossing rhine river
"miracle of remagen"
continued push toward berlin

hitler committing suicide
fuhrerbunker near chancellery
third reich defeated
may 8, 1945 v-e day
later discovering nazi camps
dachau buchenwald bergen-belsen
holocaust extermination of jews
other german enemies
allied peace disagreements
stalin building berlin wall
staring "cold war" opposition
united states armed forces
versus russian military machine
japan surprise attack
pearl harbor sunday morning bombing
beginning world war two
president roosevelt's
"a date which will live in infamy"
zero fighters and dive bombers
sinking four battleships
destroying hickham field
ford island airplane hangers
tom watching hollywood films
"wake island" "guadalcanal diary" "destination tokyo"
"they were expendable" filipino p.t. boats
pappy boyington "flying tiger" kills
john wayne's toughness in
"sands of iwo jima"
u.s.s. indianapolis
delivering atomic bomb parts
to tinian in marianas
later sunk by
japanese submarine torpedoes

few sailors rescued
following major sweeney's b-29
"fat man" detonation over nagasaki
japan surrendered to the allies
august 15, 1945
treaty signed on *u.s.s. missouri* decks
american occupation forces
eventually yielding to
honda nikon sony
economic manufacturing business trading
high school junior
missing korea by a few months
"the forgotten war"
we didn't win didn't lose
samuel fuller's black-and-white
"fixed bayonets" "the steel helmet"
bringing deaths home
high school diploma 1955
pregnant girl friend
getting married
thinking of cuba
making island plane trip
joining fidel and che
fighting from oriente province
to victory in havana streets
later college professor
with failing students
vietnam cannon fodder grunts
wife and children exemptions
too old to enlist
still could have
joined foreign journalists
covering military battles

international political details
michael herr's *dispatches*
tim page's *nam* photographs
his *page by page* military history
hue chu lain ha trang da nang
cam ranh bay china beach
smoking marijuana and opium
blackout alky ethers
wondering if sean flynn dana stone
remains will be found
discovering my true calling
deciding to write poetry
no more sixteen-year old
military establishment supporter
my idealism died in vietnam
deaths mias many wounded
sad young boys gone mad
with god silent
not saying anything
abandoning loyalty
devotion and self-sacrifice
leaving my country
becoming thief of fire
dove left wing peace-nik
poet robber gambler
seeking a new life
fresh beginning
hoping always hoping

loretta's song

awake early morning
dark black hours
moments before first light
mind fresh
sitting thinking writing
choosing autumn pilgrimage
dream walking **cliffs**
artful dodger tranny-trip
horses regularly humming
occasional rush of long white
brief flurries flying
crossing brautigan creek
fallen log bridge
steady footsteps
journeying inside myself
climbing basaltic heights
search for sanctuary over
finally home
special holy place
tree leaves rattling
like dry bones turning
cold orange harvest moon
brilliant milky way
sparkling distant stars
listening for voices
animals hiding
waiting until you pass
graybeard wisdom
entering world helpless
suddenly waking up old
soon leaving breathless

scared resigned angry
waiting god's blessing
or in larkin's
"aubabe" verse
"lost always
not to be here
not to be anywhere"
john lennon's lyrics
"imagine there's no heaven
no hell below us
above us only sky"
maybe dark womb odyssey
black tunnel
white light mystery
glorious afterlife
peaceful heaven waiting
warm reunion with
family friends relations
graying geezer
in twilight shadows
avoiding disinfectant smell
stale urine stink
fat nursing home help
smiley-faced smocks
wheelchair bed mattress prisoner
past memories
tortured hurts
marvelous celebrations
rapidly rolling by
flowing silently like ancient
black-and-white movies
thinking of close friends dead
others long forgotten

never young again
full of life's successes
or feeling
tender loving touch
hot sexual desire
memories of young jennifer
middle of the night
light rucksack
porcupine mountains path
hiking to shining clouds falls
suddenly telling me
she doesn't care anymore
painfully trying to accept
understand her rejection
girlfriend kaput
living beyond others
those who cannot love
dry fleshy wrinkles
muscles painful warp
cliffs trail without
big city asphalt
dark shadows of
tall anonymous buildings
lego mortar landscape
metropolitan cloverleafs
concrete penetrator route
connecting to downtown
masses of loud noises
high human energies
electric discordant sounds
steady thrum of voices
exciting pulsing rhythms
police car fire engines

ambulance sirens wail
in contrast
to my small metrops
fifth street main drag
personal business touch
known customers important
conglomerate café
italian ethiopian roasts
copper country art gallery
affordable computer repair
baptist store front church
"bible believing faith"
curves leveque insurance citizens bank
holistic family clinic
dollar store
thurner's bakery
copper country mission
"angel room fellowship"
cross-country sports
bikes and skis
tamarack trading post
u.p. pub
silagy's pizza works
john's family restaurant
bucko's party store
artis books and antiques
erikka's garage
red jacket general store
north end bar
keweenaw auto body
older used cars in front
no walmart shopko econo foods
office maximum

fast food mcmansions
nighttime neon hues
strip mall box stores
greedy ignorant people
dreams unfulfilled
lacking exciting adventures
endless empty cell-phone words
spending money
to end bad day blues
buying more "stuff"
to eliminate numbing boredom
those who always take
never share with others
sad bodies watching television
nothing else to do
soap operas
christian gospel shows
big bucks game contests
nascar wrestling cooking
mad folks weeping and screaming
talk show truths
someone else's reality
daily t.v. celebrity worship
fake actors real friends
weather weather weather
tornados floods blizzard storms
baby sitting channels
brain numbing advertisements
beer commercials
life health insurance plans
vitamins potato chips viagra tampax
poet quietly abandoning
wife kids house

middle-class mediocrity
same old same old
9 to 5 routines
suit white shirt power tie
attaché case toothpaste smile
office desk
pen and pencil collection
new computer technology
state of the arts coffee machine
aimless daily carpet shuffle
those without lives
surviving insane existence
no longer one of them
not like my father
emery owned
by things he possessed
tommy no dummy child
imagination fired by
chasing deep creative passions
quitting boy scouts
american nazi brain washing
not believing
"my country right or wrong"
ignoring cnn fox news
passing soundbite politics
good government citizen
filling out bureaucratic forms
obeying the ridiculous
yet critically opposing
demonstrating against
nam iraq afghanistan
violent patriotic hatreds
sundays filling churches

bible class coloring books
different crayon shades
spilling over the lines
tasting wafers
sipping cheap wine
blood of the lord
denying the resurrection
jesus in heaven with god
wanting a savior
facing society's hell
human woe and alas
satisfied with rare beauty
celebrating small victories
yet wondering
if immortality of the soul
a definite possibility
aging artist
still thinking goddamn straight
experimenting beyond
creative artistic frontiers
like french spanish cave painters
lascaux and altamira
visionary hearts minds
enduring pissant criticism
saving their history
forever wrestling rat bastard time
clocks and calendar squares
precious few moments left
other poets
suffering artistic burnout
imagination energy gone
failure grinding them down
giving in to day job

.357 solution
barrel in the mouth
unwashed old man
socks full of holes
dusty beard stubble
almost bald hairline
coaxing extra miles
ancient artful dodger tranny
pissing in the sink
chugging from milk carton
black tar espresso
wondering when
my body lying flat
mouth open wide
no words coming out
wondering who will mourn me
remember who i was
write a splake-smith eulogy
specter without bootprints
left in **cliffs** rocky scree
standing on mountaintop
bathed in growing first dawn glow
eastern horizon emerging
in bright sun rays
watching white butterfly
flitting here flying there
as murakami said
unable to remember
forgotten its search
fluttering butterfly of
william carlos williams
another lost soul
unable to speak

tell the truth
about what waits beyond
soon to fly away
while chaotic world
continues to spin